Withdrawn

D1400638

THE NEED TO KNOW LIBRARY™

EVERYTHING YOU NEED TO KNOW ABOUT IMMIGRANTS AND REFUGEES

NORMA KING

Rosen
YA™

New York

Published in 2018 by The Rosen Publishing Group, Inc.
29 East 21st Street, New York, NY 10010

Copyright © 2018 by The Rosen Publishing Group, Inc.

First Edition

All rights reserved. No part of this book may be reproduced in any form without permission in writing from the publisher, except by a reviewer.

Library of Congress Cataloging-in-Publication Data

Names: King, Norma, author.
Title: Everything you need to know about immigrants and refugees/ Norma King.
Description: New York : Rosen Publishing, 2018. | Series: The need to know library | Includes bibliographical references and index. | Audience: Grades 7–12.
Identifiers: LCCN 2017025477| ISBN 9781508176725 (library bound) | ISBN 9781508176718 (pbk.) | ISBN 9781508176749 (6 pack) Subjects: LCSH: Immigrants—Juvenile literature. | Refugees—Juvenile literature. | Emigration and immigration—Juvenile literature.Classification: LCC JV6035 .K54 2018 | DDC 305.9/06912—dc23 LC record available at https://lccn.loc.gov/2017025477

Manufactured in the United States of America

INTRODUCTION

The world cannot hide from the 244 million migrants who live in a country other than their own, nor the plight of 65.6 million of them who have been forced from their homes. Modern technology broadcasts their faces and their stories daily.

Their stories aren't so different from those of the millions who preceded them through the centuries. Theirs are stories of persecution and refuge, of want and seeking new opportunity.

Nations are founded by these opportunity seekers—by brave people searching for a place to practice their religion or build a new community.

Today, many use the conveniences of modern transportation to move from one country to another. Others flee to safer borders on foot, as humankind has always done. Some pay small fortunes to ride in a rubber raft or unseaworthy boat that may sink before they reach safety. Some desperately cling to the top of a speeding train. Some arrive at their destinations and some do not.

Why do they come?

In 1983, civil war broke out in Sudan. It is estimated that over the next few years twenty-five thousand young boys fled to safety on foot when their parents were killed. They traveled hundreds of miles—some of them as young as five. The oldest were around seventeen.

CONTENTS

Sudanese refugees leave a food distribution center during a 1984 famine that plagued Western Sudan and many other parts of Africa.

They became each other's families—bigger ones carrying the smaller ones, sharing meager food, and burying those who didn't make it.

After living as refugees in Ethiopia for about four years, war broke out there and they were forced by gunpoint to flee back to Sudan.

Thousands died trying to cross the River Gilo, where they were felled by bullets, drowned, or eaten by crocodiles.

Only about half of them—ten thousand or so— survived the journey, which led them ultimately to the Kakuma refugee camp in Kenya.

Those boys are grown now. Some still live in Kenya, some live in other countries.

But there are other boys and girls, men and women still fleeing civil war and strife.

There are others seeking to lift themselves from poverty in another nation through immigration.

They all face their crocodiles.

And they will not be ignored.

Their stories are a part of our world.

CHAPTER ONE

PEOPLE IN MOTION ON PLANET EARTH

W e often call people who move between nations immigrants and refugees. However, not everyone fits into just those two groups. There are also internally displaced persons (IDP), stateless persons, asylum seekers, and unaccompanied minors.

These categories include men, women, children, families, single people, the old, and the young. They come from many races, religions, and creeds.

Who are they? Where did they come from? Where are they now?

IMMIGRANTS

Immigrants are people who leave their country in search of better jobs and better futures, such as the Chinese who immigrated to the United States during the time of the California gold rush during the 1850s, or the Irish who fled the potato famine in Ireland about the same time.

There were few immigration laws during those times. However, today each country has its own immigration

During the Irish potato famine an estimated one million peasants died. Here, a woman gives clothing to famine victims in 1849.

laws. Undocumented immigrants do not have legal permission to live in a country. Sometimes they are referred to in a negative way as illegal immigrants or illegal aliens.

These unauthorized immigrants come for the same reason as all immigrants—a chance for better jobs and futures. They find ways to cross the borders undetected.

Many unauthorized immigrants from Mexico and Central and South America have traveled north and crossed into the United States through states that border Mexico. Some people attempting to cross are captured by border patrol agents and sent back, others are not. Some immigrants may first come into a country legally, such as on a work visa, but do not leave when their visa expires. At that point, they become undocumented immigrants.

REFUGEES AND INTERNALLY DISPLACED PERSONS

Refugees are those who flee their country because of war, persecution, famine, political upheaval, or fear of death. Refugees, such as those fleeing the civil war in Syria today, may travel on foot for days or months with little food. Others pay smugglers to get them across an ocean to what they consider a safe country. These journeys do not always end well, with boats capsizing, betrayal, and death. In 2016, at least five thousand refugees drowned in the Mediterranean, according to the United Nations (UN), as they fled countries in West Africa and the Middle East.

If refugees make it to a new country, they must apply for refugee status according to that country's laws. Many Syrians today flee to surrounding countries such as Turkey, Lebanon, Jordan, Egypt, and Iraq and end up living in refugee camps. Only a small percentage will actually be resettled in another country. International law protects refugees from being forcibly returned to their home country.

Internally displaced persons (IDP) flee their homes to avoid violence or harassment but stay in their country. Their government should protect them,

Millions of Syrians have fled their country's civil war, including this family from Aleppo who applied for asylum in Munich, Germany.

although its policies may be the reason they fled their homes to begin with. An estimated 6.6 million Syrians were displaced in their own country in 2016.

OTHERS WITHOUT A COUNTRY

Stateless people do not have citizenship in any country. The Dalai Lama, once a leader in Tibet, became stateless when he fled Tibet after a rebellion against Chinese rule failed in 1959. He, and thousands of others who followed, continue to be stateless.

There are about ten million stateless people in the world. They do not have the same rights as citizens and may be denied employment, education, and health care. They cannot own property or even travel freely. People may become stateless because of discrimination; when a nation dissolves and new nations are created; or when a country changes its nationality laws. In some countries, mothers cannot transfer their nationality to their children; in other countries, if a child's birth is not registered he or she may be considered stateless.

Perhaps the best-known stateless person is the Dalai Lama, the spiritual leader of Tibet who fled his country in 1959.

Many of the Roma people in the Balkans, who were once called gypsies (a term that is now considered a slur), cannot prove their relationship to the former republic of Yugoslavia and are considered stateless.

ASYLUM SEEKERS

Asylum seekers may either come to a new country seeking refugee status or may already be in the country as a migrant and be threatened with removal. Until an asylee (one seeking political asylum) is given refugee status, that person remains an asylum seeker. If he or she is refused asylum, the asylum seeker could be sent back to his or her home country, even though it may not be safe to return.

According to a 2015 report by the office of the United Nations High Commissioner for Refugees (UNHCR), Syrians make up the biggest group of people seeking asylum. Syrian refugees reside in 120 countries.

PEOPLE IN MOTION—HOW MANY?

Millions of people worldwide have been forced from their homes. These forcibly displaced people total 65.3 million, according to the United Nations in a 2015 report.

If the 65.3 million people were one nation, it would rank twenty-first in a ranking of the largest nations in the world and larger than Great Britain. Of that number, there are 22.5 million refugees and over half of them—51 percent—are children.

Internally displaced persons total 40.8 million. These are people who have fled their homes but still live in their home country.

Asylum seekers—those hoping to get refugee status—total 2.8 million.

Only 189,300 refugees (out of 22.5 million) were

resettled in 2016. The United States took in the highest number with 96,900.

Migrants make up 3.3 percent of the world's population, according to the UN. That means that there are 244 million immigrants in the world today who have left their home country and moved to another—some legally and some illegally.

UNACCOMPANIED MINORS

Unaccompanied minors are children or teens under the age of eighteen who have left their countries and are now alone. They hope to be given refugee status or legal immigrant status in a new country. Often they flee their country because of war, persecution, or poverty. Some from Central America have fled their home countries because they have been threatened by powerful gangs.

Many minors travel on foot. Sometimes they or their parents hire smugglers to get them across the borders.

CHAPTER TWO

REFUGEES AND IMMIGRANTS THROUGH HISTORY

Immigrants and refugees are an important part of history. Let's examine some of the groups that ultimately became part of American history.

THE HUGUENOTS

The word "refugee" comes from the French word *refuge*, which means "hiding place."

It was the French Huguenots (hue-ga-nots) during the seventeenth century who were first called refugees.

As Protestants, their religious beliefs differed from the Catholic Church and the king of France. In 1562, the conflict resulted in the French Wars of Religion, which lasted thirty-five years. These ended when Henry IV signed the Edict of Nantes in April 1598 granting religious freedoms.

However, almost one hundred years later, in 1685, King Louis XIV revoked the Edict of Nantes and hundreds of thousands of Huguenots fled France for Europe, South America, and North America. They

French Huguenots were the first to be called refugees. They were welcomed to Berlin in 1685 by Friedrich Wilhelm I of Brandenburg.

feared persecution, death, and loss of religious freedom if they stayed.

AMERICAN INDIANS

Native Americans or American Indians could be called the first immigrants to the Americas. Their descendants would later become refugees. There are many theories on how these people arrived on the American continent thousands of years ago. Some believe they crossed a land bridge from Asia to America that existed at the time; others believe they came in boats from Australia or other locations. After Europeans came to the Americas, many Native Americans were resettled on reservations so white settlers could have their lands.

The Homestead Act of 1862 opened up Indian lands in the western United States to settlers. It gave the new settlers the right to homestead on 160 acres (65 hectares), although Indians had lived on the land for generations. During the summer of 1838, about thirteen thousand Cherokee Indians in and around the Appalachian Mountains were forced to travel what is now known as the Trail of Tears to Indian Territory in Oklahoma. A military escort traveled with them those 900 miles (1,449 kilometers), not to keep them safe, but to prevent them from escaping. Conditions were bad and food was meager. More than five thousand died on this journey. Other tribes suffered similar losses as they were forced from their homes and their lands were given to settlers.

PILGRIMS

Among the best-known of the groups that settled the New World were a group who set sail from Europe in 1620.

These men, women, and children, now known as Pilgrims, left England in 1607 to find religious freedom in Holland. After living in Holland for several years, many decided to journey to the Americas. In 1620, they left Liverpool, England, for the Virginia Colonies. Due

The Pilgrims migrated to the New World in search of religious freedom. This engraving depicts their arrival at Plymouth Rock in 1620.

to bad weather, they landed on Cape Cod and later founded the Plymouth Colony on the mainland. That first winter, half of them died. The following year, one thousand Puritans left England for America, where they could practice their religion freely.

ISRAELITE AND JEWISH EXPULSION

One of the earliest records of forced migration is that of the Israelites who were expelled from Canaan in 740 BCE by the Assyrians. This land was later known as Palestine and Israel. One tribe of Israelites, the Jews,

THE EVIAN CONFERENCE, 1938

By 1938, around 150,000 German Jews had been forced out of Germany by new laws that restricted their ability to live and work. At the time, Jews were allowed to leave Germany only if they transferred their assets to the German government. But many German and Austrian Jews who fled to the United States discovered that they could not acquire the visas they needed to enter. Jewish lives were at risk, but they found they faced anti-Semitism in asylum countries as well. This was at the height of the Great Depression in the United States, and many Americans believed that letting German and Austrian Jews into the country would only add to the economic burden of the time. Britain and France appealed to the German government for the release of Jewish assets in order to provide some aid in the relocation process. Germany refused.

That summer, delegates from thirty-two countries attended the Evian Conference, which was held at a French resort of the same name. The goal of this conference was to solve the Jewish immigration issue. But even with the news of pogroms and other human rights violations against the Jews, attending countries were not all open to offering asylum.

The British delegate said that Britain was already fully populated and had high unemployment and could not take in refugees, except in small numbers in British territories in East Africa. The French delegate said that France had reached the point of extreme saturation with refugees. The delegate from the United States said the United States could only extend the unfilled immigration quota of Germans and Austrians to the Jewish refugees.

Only the tiny country of the Dominican Republic agreed to take in refugees—between fifty thousand and one hundred thousand—but many questioned the country's reasons for doing so. The Dominican Republic itself had slaughtered twenty-five thousand Haitians in 1937 in an attempt to keep Dominican men and women from marrying darker-skinned people. Many suspected that dictator Rafael Trujillo was trying to distract from that atrocity by offering asylum to German Jews. Only fifty Jews made it to the Dominican Republic in the first year of the country's immigration program.

In May 1939, the ocean liner *St. Louis* left Hamburg, Germany, with 937 Jewish refugees en route to Havana, Cuba. Passengers hoped to enter the United States after getting the proper documents in Cuba. Due to anti-Semitism in both Cuba and the United States and concerns about competition for jobs, among other factors, only twenty-two Jews, with the proper documentation, were allowed to disembark in Havana.

The *St. Louis* was forced to return to Europe.

Jewish organizations there were able to secure entry for many of the *St. Louis* refugees in safe European nations; but 254 of the original 937 Jewish refugees on the *St. Louis* died in the Holocaust.

has been the subject of persecution and expulsion many times. In the late fifteenth century, Jews were expelled from Spain when they refused to convert to Catholicism.

In 1881, Jews were blamed for the assassination of Czar Alexander in Russia and fled that country to avoid the pogroms—organized persecution. An estimated two million Jews immigrated to the United States between

Lord Winterton of England spoke at the Evian Conference in 1938 on the Jewish refugee crisis prior to the start of World War II.

1881 and 1914. Others immigrated to countries in Latin America, Europe, and Palestine.

The best-known migration of Jews happened before, during, and after World War II when they fled Germany and German-occupied territory to avoid genocide carried out by the regime of Adolf Hitler and the Nazi Party.

IRISH IMMIGRANTS

Irish immigrants began to settle in America as far back as the 1600s. In the 1840s, a famine in Ireland caused a mass exodus of peasants. Irish peasants

ANNIE MOORE, FIRST TO DISEMBARK AT ELLIS ISLAND

Annie Moore, trailed by her two younger brothers, was the first immigrant to set foot on Ellis Island, the immigrant station in Upper New York Bay, in early January 1892.

The three Moore siblings hailed from County Cork, Ireland. Just twelve days earlier, they had boarded the SS *Nevada* in Queenstown. Annie, seventeen, and her brothers, Anthony, eleven, and Phillip, seven, were reunited with their parents, who had come to New York three years earlier and worked to save money to bring their children over.

From the time Annie arrived in the United States in 1892 to the closing of the immigration center in 1954, over twelve million immigrants entered the United States at Ellis Island. However, not all immigrants at Ellis Island were allowed to stay. Between 1892 and 1924, 2 percent were sent back to their home country because of health concerns or because inspectors thought the person would become dependent upon society.

relied on potatoes as their main food. However, from 1845 to 1850 there was no potato crop. An estimated one million people died of starvation and disease. Many landowners were anxious to get rid of the starving peasants. They paid for their passage across the Atlantic to Canada and the United States. By the end of 1854, two million Irish had immigrated to America. Once in America, many workers were able to find jobs.

CHAPTER THREE

MODERN-DAY REFUGEES AND IMMIGRANTS

International migrants, or those living in a different country from their birth, totaled 244 million in 2016, according to the United Nations.

Immigrants—those voluntarily leaving their home countries to live in another country—do so to join family members, get better jobs, and have more opportunities. Some apply to enter the new country legally, and others seek to cross borders and enter as undocumented immigrants.

Many arrive with little or nothing. The biggest challenge they face is a new language. Even if they have the help of friends or family who speak the language, just doing basic things like signing a lease, applying for a job, enrolling children in school, or getting public assistance can be hard.

The language barrier prevents immigrants from integrating into their new communities, communicating with teachers, doctors, police, coworkers, employers, and many others. Because children and teens are enrolled in school, they often learn the language more quickly—although they may have challenges in school and fall behind their classmates.

These two Syrian refugees are enrolled in an English as a Second Language (ESL) class in San Diego, California. Many refugees work to learn the primary language of their new country.

Adult immigrants and refugees are encouraged to enroll in language classes in their new country. Attending the classes may be difficult because of work schedules or transportation issues.

Supporting themselves and their families in a new country is often a challenge. When immigrants and refugees find work—unless they are entering the country on a work visa for a specific industry—they are usually employed in low-paying jobs because of the language problem. Even if the immigrant had a skill or certification in their old country, they may not be able to

ADVICE FOR TEENAGE IMMIGRANTS

Moving to a new country is not easy. Teen migrants leave family, friends, jobs, schools, and their culture behind. Most will have to learn a new language. Many will be subject to discrimination.

Teens can be successful in their new countries by working hard to get a good education. It's important to attend school, study hard, and move on from high school to higher education opportunities.

Falling in with the wrong crowd and making bad decisions will handicap a teen's future. Teens should get involved with groups that help immigrant teens with after-school programs such as tutoring, counseling, life-skills training, and recreational activities.

Immigrants can take steps to overcome discrimination by educating others about their culture. An immigrant teen featured in the Huffington Post, Jessica Hernandez, shared these tips for others: "Be patient and don't give up; be kind, treat others with respect; don't judge others; and remember everyone is an immigrant."

"Teens should follow their own dreams," said Bob Ponichtera, executive director and founder of Liberty's Promise, a nonprofit that helps immigrant teens adjust to life in the United States. Teens should not be pressured to follow their parents' expectations.

Being an immigrant has made her stronger, said Jessica. "It taught me how to be determined, work twice as hard, and overcome obstacles."

work in the same field in the new country. Certifications don't transfer between countries. A woman who was a nurse in Uruguay found the only work she could get in the United States was as a nanny and housekeeper.

Some employers take advantage of immigrants who are anxious to work but unable to get a job because of language or certifications. The workers may be exploited or be given dangerous or undesirable work for very low pay. Undocumented workers will often take whatever job is offered for whatever pay they can get.

Transportation has its own set of challenges to newcomers to a country. Tasks as simple as crossing the street or catching a bus become difficult for an

Many refugees and immigrants must take work in low-paying jobs such as hotel housekeeping because of language barriers.

immigrant who can't read street signs or bus schedules or who doesn't understand traffic lights and crosswalks.

Cultural differences are many and can range from the roles of mothers and fathers to dress, observance of holidays, and foods. Even different weather in a new country can cause stress for a migrant.

One Utah church youth group invited refugee teens to join them for a weeklong hiking trip as an effort to form friendships between the two groups of teens. The hike turned out to be a disaster when "…less than a day into the hike, some of the refugee kids became very upset. The hike, it turned out, had reminded them of the time when they were forced to flee their homes. Now, despite the group's kindest intentions, these kids were being retraumatized," wrote Christina Nuñez in Global Citizen.

Housing can be difficult because of the meager income many immigrant and refugee families make. Often two or three families will live together in an apartment or house to save money. Some landlords take advantage of immigrants and refugees by offering poorly maintained facilities and high rents.

One Somalian father in Minneapolis hid his youngest child from authorities for two years so he wouldn't have to rent a larger apartment, as required by city zoning laws. He was already paying 60 percent of his income toward his rent and couldn't afford any more, according to Living in America, a study by the Robert Wood Johnson Foundation.

Sometimes parents find their own culture's traditions being swept aside by the new culture. Children

Good housing can be a problem for many migrants. Often, multiple families will share a home or an apartment to save money. Some US cities are developing housing programs to help with the process.

become "Americanized" and want to do whatever their American counterparts do.

LEAVING STREET GANGS

Thousands of youth and their families have immigrated to Mexico and the United States after being terrorized by gangs in what is known as the Northern Triangle: Guatemala, El Salvador, and Honduras. These powerful gangs have gained power through extortion, robbery, and kidnapping.

One Salvadoran girl, fifteen-year-old Maribel, told a reporter for the UN, that she and her family fled after she was threatened by Barrio 18 gang members.

"It is better to have nothing to do with the gangs. But it can be hard to keep them out of your life," she says. "They feel immune because they have guns and people are scared of them. They think they can kill who they like, and they can rape who they like."

A teenage boy said he was beaten by a gang and then told he had passed their initiation and was now a member. "I left my mom's house the very next day and stayed with a family friend across the city. If I had gone back to the barrio and refused to be in the gang, they would have killed me," he said.

In 2015, according to the UNHCR, 110,000 people fled the Northern Triangle to find asylum in Mexico, Costa Rica, the United States, and other countries in the region.

MYTHS AND FACTS

MYTH: Refugees are terrorists.

FACT: Refugees are often fleeing terrorist groups such as ISIS and Boko Haram, which threaten the peace and security of their country.

MYTH: Refugees who come to the United States are all Muslim.

FACT: Of the 84,995 refugees resettled in the United States in fiscal year 2016, 46 percent were Muslim and 44 percent were Christian.

MYTH: Most refugees are men.

FACT: More than half of the world's refugees are children under the age of eighteen.

CHAPTER FOUR

THE PLIGHT OF IMMIGRANTS

Many people in the Americas are descendants of immigrants. Some were searching for religious freedom, some were looking for new lives and opportunities, some were explorers, and some were indentured servants.

The largest South American country, Brazil, was discovered by a Portuguese explorer, Pedro Álvares Cabral, in 1500. He was on an expedition to India for King Manuel I of Portugal. He claimed the land for Portugal, although it was inhabited by Native Americans.

Australia was settled by Great Britain as a penal colony for convicts. Its first people were Aboriginal Australians, who had come from South Asia. In 1788, British ships brought 751 English convicts to Australia. About one-fifth of the convicts were women. The total number of convicts sent to Australia between 1788 and 1868 was 165,000.

MIGRATION TODAY

Today, there are millions of people migrating to homes in other countries. Migrants may be immigrants or emigrants. "Emigrant" is the word describing a person who leaves the country of his or her birth. When emigrants arrive in a new country, they are called immigrants. Sometimes refugees are referred to as immigrants.

There were 244 million immigrants scattered throughout the world in 2016, according to the United Nations. Most are from India, then Mexico, followed by the Russian Federation.

Pedro Alvares Cabral claimed Brazil for Portugal in 1500 while on a quest to find India, opening that country to Portuguese immigration.

Nearly two-thirds of these migrants live in Europe or Asia, and most come from a country in the same region. The majority of immigrants are men, at 51.8 percent. Most are of working age.

WHY DO THEY COME?

In many parts of the world, immigration is one of the few options for people, particularly young people, to find decent work and escape poverty in their home countries. They may seek better health care or better opportunities for their children. Some want to join family members who have already immigrated. Some immigrants are highly skilled and invited by companies to come and work in a new country.

Green card holders are immigrants who have been given legal permission to live in the United States. They can live and work anywhere in the United States, own property, attend school, join the military, and apply to be a US citizen.

Only a limited number of green cards are available each year. They may be given to relatives of permanent residents or to preferred job holders. Some are awarded by lottery. The green card lottery is officially known as the Diversity Immigrant Visa Program. Which nationalities can apply for the program changes each year. Only fifty thousand winners are chosen each year.

UNAUTHORIZED IMMIGRANTS

The Department of Homeland Security (DHS) apprehended 462,388 undocumented immigrants in 2015 in the United States. Perhaps one-third to one-half of undocumented immigrants had visas at one time and failed to return to their home country when the visa expired.

Unauthorized immigrants have been referred to in many ways. Sometimes negative words such as "illegals" or "illegal aliens" are used to refer to those who come into a country without taking proper legal steps. They may have joined family members who were already in that country (whether legal or not) or they may have been on their own. They all came for simi-

THE TERRIFYING TRIP NORTH

For a number of years, Central Americans fleeing violence and poverty in their homelands have braved the challenges of La Bestia—or "The Beast."

La Bestia is the name given to freight trains, which travel from the southern to the northern border of Mexico, taking goods to the United States. The trains are not meant for passengers, but many migrants jump aboard and ride on top.

The trip north is dangerous in many ways. Migrants falling from the roofs of the trains may suffer serious injuries or amputations. Gangs often infiltrate groups of migrants and demand ransom, sell drugs, trick girls into prostitution, and lure boys into joining the gangs. Sometimes, if passengers are unwilling to pay the ransom, they are thrown off the speeding train by gang members.

In 2014, the Mexican government announced measures to keep the migrants off the trains: building walls near areas where the trains slowed to prevent people from jumping on the train, increasing the speed of the train, and increased numbers of police and immigration agents patrolling train stations.

These measures have cut down on the numbers jumping the trains but migrants are still making the journey into Mexico and on to the US border. Many of them are unaccompanied minors—youth under the age of eighteen—who travel without their families.

Now some migrants take other routes, walking through the mountains, crossing rivers, or employing smugglers.

(continued on the next page)

(continued from the previous page)

There are safe houses and sympathetic Mexicans who try to help the migrants. But, in many ways, the new routes are more dangerous than La Bestia. Some of the migrants are apprehended by police, some fall into the clutches of gangs, some are killed by robbers, some are kidnapped. And some make it to the United States.

lar reasons: seeking a better life or fleeing poverty or persecution in their home country.

DREAMERS

In 2012, President Barack Obama signed the Deferred Action for Childhood Arrivals (DACA). This executive action protects undocumented immigrant youth who came to the United States as children from deportation and gives them a work permit for two years. These youth, DREAMers as they have been called, can apply for DACA status between the ages of fourteen and thirty-one. Their status can be renewed every two years.

However, in September 2017, the Trump administration announced that DACA would end in six months' time, with the understanding that Congress could use those six months to determine a legislative solution. An estimated 750,000 youth and young adults had DACA status in 2017. A few have been arrested and threatened with deportation.

In February 2015, US president Barack Obama spoke to young immigrants about the Deferred Action for Child Arrivals (DACA) policy, which gives them relief from deportation.

A FAMILY FLEES THE MIDDLE EAST

When Ibraheem Alkhwaja learned his family had been approved for resettlement in the United States, he was afraid. "We heard that the United States of America was one of the mafia gangs," said Alkhwaja.

However, after arriving in the United States in September 2016, he discovered that the TV shows he'd seen in Syria and Jordan, such as *Walker, Texas Ranger* and *The Sopranos*, did not depict true

American life. The six-member family was well treated by the placement agency and their new neighbors.

The Syrian civil war broke out in 2011. Ibraheem (E-brah-heem) and Enas (E-naw-s) and their three sons, Faras, Ammar, and Hamseh, lived in Ghouta, Syria, where Ibraheem worked in construction and drove trucks and a taxi. (Later, a fourth son would be born in Jordan.)

On the day the war spread to Ghouta in 2013, the family fled the city. Ibraheem went back later to check their home and was shot four times by a sniper. Fortunately, none of his injuries was life threatening.

Their house, their mosque, and the school had been destroyed.

They lived with family and friends until Ibraheem hired a guide, or smuggler, for 60,000 Lebanese pounds (around $600 USD) to take them to the Syria-Jordan border. The guide, Ivan, took the family and ten other people in a van through the desert to reach the border. Along the way, they detoured to avoid a vehicle that had been hit with a missile. They ended up at the Zaatari refugee camp in Jordan, where officials confiscated everyone's ID and their official Family Books, issued by the Syrian government. An overwhelming sixty thousand Syrians were living in tents in Zaatari, which Ibraheem viewed as a fire hazard.

Enas wanted to go back to Syria, "Very bad Zaatari," she recalled.

They stayed only one night in the dusty, hot, mosquito-infested camp before they fled.

At 7 a.m. the second day, when the gates at the camp opened for a water truck, a friend's smaller truck came in, too. The families jumped into the back, put a blanket over their heads, and headed out. They traveled through the desert toward Amman, the capital of Jordan.

Ibraheem found a job driving a dump truck for a mining company in the desert. And Feras went to a Jordanian school.

Jordanian children weren't kind to the Syrian boy. "My son didn't like to go," said Enas. "Jordanian kids threw feces, rocks [on his way] to school."

After three months, they were able to get new IDs and register as refugees with the UN.

It was January 2016 when they got the call telling them they were being considered for resettlement. Ibraheem and Enas traveled hours to Amman to be interviewed by an officer. They returned about ten more times for more interviews. In August 2016, they learned they had been approved for resettlement in Kansas City, Missouri.

On September 21, they arrived at Kansas City International Airport at noon. No one was there to meet them. Their plane itinerary had changed, and Della Lamb Community Services, the agency that was handling their resettlement, was expecting them at midnight. Eventually, the family was picked up and taken to their new home in Independence, Missouri.

That first night, Ibraheem was still scared about his new country. He stayed awake worrying that someone would try to break into the house. The next day, he walked through his new neighborhood and saw that it was an ordinary place with children playing in their yard, dogs barking, and friendly people. He felt better.

In early 2017, US president Donald Trump signed executive orders temporarily halting refugee resettlement in the United States.

With their families still in Syria, their neighbors have become like family, say Enas and Ibraheem. One neighbor helped Ibraheem get a job in construction, others have given rides, taken the boys fishing, translated their mail, and become friends.

"I have not seen trouble for God has given me sustenance in neighbors," says Ibraheem.

EXECUTIVE ORDERS

In 2016, the UN estimated that there were 22.5 million refugees. Only 189,300 were resettled that year—that's less than 1 percent. The remaining 22.3 million were hosted in refugee camps and similar situations, most in developing nations.

These host countries "bear the brunt of the response to the Syrian crisis in a manner that is not sustainable, and may ultimately generate further instability," said Kelly Clements, United Nations deputy high commissioner for refugees, during a conference on refugees.

World leaders have responded in different ways to the refugee crisis. In 2016, members of the European Union, concerned about Syrian refugees fleeing across the Aegean Sea to Greece, where they would then pass into different countries in Europe, reached an agreement with Turkey to continue to host these refugees, with financial assistance coming from the European Union. Greece also committed to returning any refugees who made the dangerous crossing by boat back to Turkey.

In the United States, President Donald Trump, who took office in January 2017, issued an executive order on March 6, 2017, temporarily halting any refugee resettlement in the country for 120 days. After July 14, refugees who were already approved for resettlement may be required to go through new background and security checks before coming to the United States.

Some nations are concerned that refugees will increase the likelihood of terrorist incidents. In particular, they point to refugees from Syria and Iraq as a possible source of terrorism. People who have a negative view of Muslims are more likely to fear refugee entry into their countries, according to a survey done in ten European Union nations by Pew Research in 2016. Others are concerned that refugee assistance will drain the resources of their countries and affect the well-being of their own citizens.

Still, there are many people and nations interested in helping refugees. Thirty countries throughout the world have refugee resettlement programs. The UNHCR operated on a $7.5 billion a year budget in 2016, most of which was voluntary contributions. Governments and the European Union donate 86 percent of its budget; 6 percent comes from other government organizations; 6 percent comes from private donations, including foundations, corporations, and

Representatives from many countries gather in Brussels, Belgium, in April 2017 to discuss humanitarian relief for Syrians. Donors pledged $6 billion for relief efforts.

the public. Two percent of UNHCR's money comes from the UN for administrative costs.

During the 2017 Brussels Conference on Supporting Syria, donors pledged an additional $6 billion to provide humanitarian assistance in Syria and nearby countries. An additional $3.7 billion was pledged for 2018 and beyond to help refugees, those inside Syria, and countries hosting refugees. More will be needed.

Countries with resettlement programs provide financial resources to help the refugees for a limited time. Many churches and agencies recognize the needs refugees have and provide services for them. This is usually given at no cost to the refugees themselves.

CHAPTER FIVE

HELPING REFUGEES TODAY

R efugees are among the most vulnerable people in the world, says António Guterres, who was the United Nations high commissioner for refugees from 2002 until 2015.

The first refugees of the twentieth century fled their countries during and after World War I. It is estimated that 7.5 million people were displaced after World War I. After World War II, millions more people became refugees. In 1950, the United Nations created the office of the United Nations High Commissioner of Refugees (UNHCR).

The UNHCR's mission is to make sure that the rights of refugees are protected and oversee resettlement efforts in other countries. More than nine hundred non-governmental organizations (NGOs) throughout the world assist in relief and resettlement efforts.

WHERE DO REFUGEES FLEE?

When refugees flee their homes, they often take little or nothing with them. They may travel by foot, in vehicles,

Refugees from Europe arrive in New York on the SS *Ernie Pyle* in September 1947 to start a new life in America.

or even try a water crossing to a safer country. At the border, they may be stopped by police or other law enforcement personnel and taken to a refugee camp. Sometimes they travel alone, other times they are with family or groups of people. Many hire smugglers to get them to a safer country.

A huge number of refugees—68 percent—live in refugee camps in the Middle East and Africa. Unfortunately, less than 1 percent of refugees will ever be resettled in another country. In 2016, there were thirty-seven host countries willing to accept refugees. The countries that took the most refugees in 2016 were the United States, with 78,340 new refugees; Canada, with 21,838 new refugees; the UK, with 5,074; and Australia, with 7,502 new refugees.

REFUGEE WATER CROSSINGS

Many refugees fled by sea following the Vietnam War in the 1970s. Tens of thousands of Vietnamese attempted to cross the South China Sea to Malaysia, Hong Kong, the Philippines, and other countries. Many became victims of pirates who attacked and disabled their boats, robbed them, and sometimes killed them. Sometimes the survivors were picked up by merchant ships. As the numbers of Vietnamese boat people, as they were called, rose, countries became overwhelmed and refused to allow the refugees on land. The UNHCR stepped in to deal with these problems and make sure merchant ships were reimbursed.

Refugees have fled on boats from Haiti and Cuba to Florida for decades. In April 1980, 125,000 Cubans fled when the government allowed a brief six-month window.

During 2015, more than one million refugees tried to cross the Mediterranean or Aegean Seas to Greece and Italy. About 3,770 attempting to cross the Mediterranean Sea to Europe were drowned or were reported missing.

In 2016, an agreement between the European Union and Turkey reduced the numbers of refugees trying to cross the Aegean Sea by 98 percent. The agreement required Greece to return all water refugees who made

Many refugees today, just like these Cuban refugees in 1994, often attempt dangerous water crossings to find a new home.

it to Greece back to Turkey, in return for financial assistance and other concessions.

In the first three months of 2017, it is estimated that 798 migrants died during water crossings on the Mediterranean. In three days in April 2017, five thousand refugees were rescued.

Water rescues are done by the Italian coast guard, Frontex (the EU's border patrol agency), and humanitarian groups. Groups such as Migrant Offshore Aid Station (MOAS) and Sea-Watch use radar, drones, and satellite imagery to find refugee boats. Some government officials are concerned that the presence of these NGOs increases the likelihood of refugee boats being launched.

THE MISSION OF UNHCR

In 1921, the fledgling League of Nations created the first refugee aid system to assist refugees from European countries following World War I.

Then in 1950, the United Nations, which had replaced the League of Nations, created the United Nations High Commissioner of Refugees (UNHCR) to lead efforts worldwide to protect refugees and help them. At that time, many thought it would take only three years to solve the refugee problem and at that point the UNHCR could be disbanded. Now, more than six decades later, the refugees' numbers are still growing, and the UNHCR is still an important organization.

The UNHCR ensures that refugees can seek asylum and find refuge in another country. At a conference in 1951, the Convention Relating to the Status of Refugees was created. It was an agreement that refugees should be treated as well as any other foreigner in a country and in many cases, as well as a citizen of the country. It also assigns responsibilities for the refugee to the host country.

The convention was created to protect refugees following World War II. Later, the 1967 Protocol was approved, which expanded the convention's rights and responsibilities to all refugees. One hundred forty-eight countries have agreed to the convention and its protocol.

An important right given by the convention was non-refoulement, which means that refugees should not be returned to the country from which they fled and where they face serious threats to their lives or freedoms.

(continued on the next page)

(continued from the previous page)

The convention outlines other rights of refugees, such as the right not to be expelled; the right not to be punished for illegal entry into a country; the right to work; the rights to housing, education, access to courts, public relief, and assistance; freedom of religion, ability to move within a country, and to be issued identity documents.

REFUGEE CAMPS

Refugee camps host hundreds of thousands of people. The top six hosting countries host about seven million refugees. Refugees live in tents or metal huts that spread out as far as the eye can see. Food is provided but usually not enough to fill basic requirements. Water is also limited, and sometimes refugees walk miles to find water each day.

About half of the refugee children are able to attend school in a refugee camp or in the hosting countries. Only about 22 percent of high school-age refugees attend school.

The four camps with the highest number of refugees are all in Kenya, in East Africa. They are:

- Kakuma refugee camp, 184,550 people, mostly South Sudanese and Somali people.
- Hagadera refugee camp, 105,998 people.
- Dagahaley refugee camp, 87,223 people.
- Ifo, 84,089 people. It has been called insanely overcrowded.

Kakuma refugee camp in Kenya, Africa, had over 184,550 refugees in 2016, most from Ethiopia, South Sudan, and Somalia.

The fifth-most-populated camp is in Zaatari, Jordan. It is home to more than 80,128 refugees, most from nearby Syria. The camp has two hospitals, nine schools, and thousands of refugee-owned shops. It also has a circus academy and a soccer league.

Yida, South Sudan, had 70,331 refugees in 2015. Its refugees are mostly Sudanese who have fled civil war. It is a haphazard, unplanned settlement.

One of the oldest refugee camps is in Katumba, Tanzania, where 66,416 live. It dates back to 1972, when Burundian refugees fled mass exterminations in their home country.

TWELVE WAYS YOU CAN HELP REFUGEES

- Find your closest refugee voluntary agency (VOLAG) online and search their website for volunteer needs. Contact the agency and get involved. Anything you can do helps, big or small.
- Agencies welcome donations of money, household items, and clothing. What can you donate? Invite your friends to donate, too.
- Welcome refugees when they arrive at airports with signs and smiles.
- Help set up a house for new refugees. This involves cleaning, stocking cupboards, making beds, arranging furniture, and making their new home attractive and livable. The VOLAG will provide donated items for the home.
- Hold a drive for clothing, books, and supplies.
- With adults, mentor a refugee family by regularly meeting with them and teaching them how to do things they aren't familiar with.
- Refugee and immigrant children attend schools and like anyone else, need friends and help with lessons and language. Be a friend.
- Help with a refugee community garden or start a community garden.
- Encourage business owners to hire refugees and immigrants to work for them.
- Stay informed about the challenges to refugees and immigrants. Read the newspapers, search online, watch news broadcasts.

- Find out what your local, state, and national elected officials are saying and doing about the refugee crisis and share your opinions.
- Learn about the cultures of refugees and immigrants, attend their public events, and make more friends.

VETTING REFUGEES

Perhaps the biggest misconception people have about refugees is that many refugees coming from the Middle East are terrorists. Since September 11, 2001, Muslims have faced this type of speculation when trying to immigrate to the United States.

The vetting, or approval, process for citizens of Middle Eastern or majority-Muslim countries to come to the United States is tortuous, with multiple screenings, interviews, and background checks, according to Natasha Hall, a former US immigration officer in Istanbul, Turkey. Hall writes in the *Washington Post* that the average wait time for refugee resettlement is eighteen to twenty-four months; while Iraqis and Syrians typically wait many years.

Two executive orders signed in early 2017 by US president Donald Trump suspended refugee admissions for six months and cut the number of refugees allowed into the United States for resettlement in half. "Whoever wrote the initial order in January 2017 must not have been aware of the screenings and procedures already used," said Hall.

The process usually starts with interviews by the UNHCR, background checks, and iris scans of the eye, which are done to create a biological identity. Then the UNHCR decides if a candidate is suitable for resettlement. Another agency steps in to collect documents and do more interviews, always looking carefully for discrepancies or possible threats in the refugees' stories.

"In the case of US resettlements, Homeland Security then conducts extensive interviews of the refugees who once again must tell their stories of persecution and escape, a process that is often traumatizing and brutal," said Hall.

One refugee, Berivan, was horribly persecuted and mistreated in Syria "in ways too horrifying to mention," wrote Hall. After being interviewed for reset-

Zeta Sarkis (*center*) and her two daughters, Anita Jnonan (*left*) and Lucine Jnonan (*right*), were among the first refugees from Iraq taken in by Germany in 2009.

tlement, Berivan was called back for another interview but instead risked her life on a rickety boat to reach Europe, rather than go through another traumatizing interview. Berivan and her husband are now making a new life in Germany, "but the United States lost a hero," said Hall.

After initial interviews, the US Citizenship and Immigration Services (USCIS) does more screenings behind the scene. In one case, a report on a refugee noted that the refugee had handed someone a piece of fruit at a checkpoint. The incident had to be investigated to determine if the refugee had "provided material support to a potential terrorist organization," wrote Hall.

Some refugees begin the application process directly with a US Resettlement Support Center (RSC) if they are relatives of asylees or refugees already in the United States.

Nine resettlement agencies in the United States work with refugees and other NGOs to resettle refugees throughout the United States. Refugee travel expenses are provided as a loan, with refugees paying the expenses back—in monthly installments—once they are settled in the new country. In 2016, the United States accepted 84,995 refugees from around the world.

10 GREAT QUESTIONS TO ASK A SPECIALIST ON IMMIGRANTS AND REFUGEES

1. What are different countries doing to help refugees and immigrants?
2. Why do refugees and unauthorized immigrants take such risks?
3. Why do religious beliefs create turmoil and war in countries?
4. Should unaccompanied minors be allowed to stay in the United States because it is not safe to return home?
5. Why must refugees live in refugee camps?
6. Should undocumented immigrants be allowed to stay in the United States?
7. Do immigrants and refugees affect me?
8. Do undocumented immigrants get welfare benefits and free healthcare?
9. Are medical and education expenses of immigrants and refugees a burden on the nation?
10. Should immigrants and refugees have to learn the language of their new country?

asylee Someone who seeks refuge or protection outside his or her home country.

Convention Relating to the Status of Refugees A document outlining the rights of refugees internationally up to 1950 and the obligations refugees have to countries where they find refuge.

DACA Stands for Deferred Action for Childhood Arrivals. An executive order that protects undocumented immigrant youth who came to the United States as children from deportation and gives them a work permit for two years.

displaced person Someone who has fled his or her home due to persecution or violence and lives in another part of that person's home country.

DREAMers Undocumented immigrants in the United States who have applied for DACA.

emigrants People who leave their country to travel to another country to live.

immigrants People living in a country that is not the country of their birth.

iris scans A highly accurate form of biometrics that creates a form of identification for individuals superior to fingerprints. Used as part of the vetting process for refugee identification.

mandate Mission or guideline for action.

migrant A general term to describe people moving across country borders to live in a country that is not of their birth. They may be immigrants, asylees, or refugees.

1967 Protocol A document amending the Convention Relating to the Status of Refugees to include all refugees after 1950.

refugees People who flee a foreign country or power to escape danger or persecution.

smuggler Someone hired to help a migrant leave his or her country and enter another country, often illegally.

state Another word for country.

stateless A person who is not a citizen of any country.

undocumented immigrants Those who are living in a country different from the one they were born in who have not taken the proper legal steps to enter the country.

United Nations An organization of 193 countries founded in 1945.

United Nations High Commissioner for Refugees (UNHCR) This name indicates both a designated person and the organization, which was created in 1950 by the United Nations to help refugees throughout the world.

vetting process A lengthy process to determine if a refugee is suitable for resettlement in another country. It includes interviews, biological screenings, and background checks by multiple agencies.

Zaatari The site of a refugee camp in Jordan that had eighty thousand people living in it in tents in 2017.

Canadian Council for Refugees (CCR)
6839 Drolet #301
Montréal, Québec, H2S 2T1
Canada
514-277-7223
Website: http://ccrweb.ca
Facebook: @ccrweb
Twitter: @ccrweb
The Canadian Council for Refugees is made up of
    organizations involved in the settlement, sponsor-
    ship, and protection of refugees and immigrants.
    The CCR sponsors a Newcomer Youth Civic
    Engagement (NYCE) Project, which helps refugee
    and immigrant youth connect with and engage with
    their communities.

Della Lamb Community Services
500 Woodland Avenue
Kansas City, MO 64106
816-842-8040
Website: http://www.dellalamb.org
Della Lamb Community Services provides resettle-
    ment services for refugees as an affiliate agency
    of the Ethiopian Community Development Counsel,
    a VOLAG (voluntary agency) approved by the US
    State Department Bureau of Population, Refugees,
    and Migration (PRM).

Ethiopian Community Development Council (ECDC)
901 South Highland Street
Arlington VA, 22204
703-685-0510
Website: http://www.ecdcus.org/
Facebook: @ECDUS.org
Twitter: @ECDC_ACC_WMA
Ethiopian Community Development Council is one
    of ten VOLAGs that receives refugee cases from
    the US State Department Bureau of Population,
    Refugees, and Migration and reassigns them to
    agency-affiliates in the United States.

Immigration and Refugee Board of Canada
Minto Place, Canada Building
344 Slater Street, 12th Floor
Ottawa, Ontario
Canada
K1A 0K1
613-995-6486
Website: http://www.irb-cisr.gc.ca/
The Immigration and Refugee Board of Canada hears
    refugee claims and determines if persons can be
    designated a refugee and remain in Canada. The
    board conducts reviews and hears appeals on
    refugee matters.

United Nations High Commissioner for Refugees
    (UNHCR)
Case Postale 2500
CH-1211 Genève 2 Dépôt

Suisse
+41 22 739 8111
Website: http://www.unhcr.org
Facebook: @UNHCR
Twitter: @refugees
Instagram: @unrefugees/
YouTube: @United Nations High Commissioner for
    Refugees (UNHCR)
The UNHCR works to protect and assist refugees
    around the world. It works with nine hundred
    VOLAGS (voluntary agencies) to assist and
    provide for the resettlement of refugees throughout
    the world.

World Relief
7 East Baltimore Street
Baltimore, MD 21202
443-451-1900
Website: https://www.worldrelief.org/
Facebook: @worldrelief
Twitter: @WorldRelief
Instagram: @worldrelief
World Relief works with churches and others to provide
    services to refugees and immigrants throughout
    the world.

Bassoff, Leah, and Laura DeLuca. *Lost Girl Found.* Berkeley, CA: House of Anansi Press, 2014.

Dublin, Thomas. *Immigrant Voices.* Urbana IL: University of Illinois Press, 2014.

Fleming, Melissa. *A Hope More Powerful Than the Sea.* New York, NY: Flatiron Books, 2017.

Kingsley, Patrick. *The New Odyssey.* New York, NY: Liveright Publishing Corporation, 2017.

Lomon, Lopez, and Mark Tabb. *Running for My Life.* Nashville, TN: Thomas Nelson, 2012.

McDonald-Gibson, Charlotte. *Cast Away.* New York, NY: The New Press, 2016.

Osborne, Linda Barrett. *This Land Is Our Land.* New York, NY: Abrams Books, 2016.

Pinkney, Andrea D. *The Red Pencil.* New York, NY: Little, Brown Books, 2014.

Rawlence, Ben. *City of Thorns: Nine Lives in the World's Largest Refugee Camp.* New York, NY: Picador, 2017.

Sepetys, Ruta. *Salt to the Sea.* New York, NY: Philomel Books, 2016.

Staley, Erin. *I'm an Undocumented Immigrant, Now What?* New York, NY: Rosen Publishing, 2017.

Alkhwaja, Ibraheem. Personal interview. April 9, 2017.

BBC News. "Syria: The Story of the Conflict." BBC.com, March 11, 2016. http://www.bbc.com/news/world -middle-east-26116868.

Chalabi, Mona. "History's Refugees." *Guardian,* July 25, 2013. https://www.theguardian.com/news /datablog/interactive/2013/jul/25/what-happened -history-refugees#Israelites.

Connor, Phillip, and Jens Manuel Krogstad. "5 Facts About the Global Somali Diaspora." Pew Research Center, June 1, 2016. http://www.pewresearch.org /fact-tank/2016/06/01/5-facts-about-the-global -somali-diaspora/.

Connor, Phillip. "International Migration: Key Findings from the U.S., Europe and the World." Pew Research Center, December 15, 2016. http://www.pewresearch.org/fact-tank/2016/12/15 /international-migration-key-findings-from-the -u-s-europe-and-the-world/.

European Commission. "EU-Turkey Statement: Questions and Answers." Fact Sheet, March 19, 2016. http://europa.eu/rapid/press-release_MEMO -16-963_en.htm.

Hadjicostis, Menelaos, and Raf Casert. "European Union Strikes Deal with Turkey to Send Back Refugees." Associated Press, March 18, 2016. http:// globalnews.ca/news/2586206/european-union -strikes-deal-with-turkey-to-send-back-refugees.

Hall, Natasha. "Refugees Are Already Vigorously Vetted. I Know Because I Vetted Them." *Washington Post*, February 1, 2017. https://www.washingtonpost.com/posteverything/wp/2017//02/01/refugees-are-already-vigorously-vetted-i-know-because-i-vetted-them/?utm_term=.ceb423708049.

Hernandez, Jessica, and Jane Bianchi. "Jessica Is an Immigrant." Huffington Post, November 20, 2013. http://www.huffingtonpost.com/2013/11/20/jessica-is-an-immigrant_n_4304636.html.

Marcovitz, Hal. "Chapter 1: The First Arrivals." Ellis Island 8. Book Collection. 2003. EBSCOhost, accessed April 23, 2017.

Nuñez, Christina. "The 7 Biggest Challenges Facing Refugees and Immigrants in the US." Global Citizen, December 12, 2014. https://www.globalcitizen.org/en/content/the-7-biggest-challenges-facing-refugees-and-immig.

Robert Wood Johnson Foundation. "Living in America: Challenges Facing New Immigrants and Refugees." August 2006. http://www.rwjf.org/content/dam/farm/reports/reports/2006/rwjf13807.

UNHCR. "Figures at a Glance." Retrieved April 23, 2017. http://www.unhcr.org/en-us/figures-at-a-glance.html.

UNRWA. "Palestine Refugees." Retrieved May 2, 2017. https://www.unrwa.org/palestine-refugees.

U.S. Refugee Admissions Program. U.S. Department of State. Retrieved May 2, 2017. https://www.state.gov/j/prm/ra/admissions/.

ABOUT THE AUTHOR

Norma King is a graduate of Brigham Young University and a writer in Kansas City, Missouri. She has written hundreds of news articles and features and enjoys dabbling in short stories and paranormal fiction. In her spare time, she works at a library, geocaches with her husband, Nick, and tries to keep up with her seventeen grandchildren.

PHOTO CREDITS

Cover Take a Pix Media/Blend Images/Getty Images; back cover Photo by Marianna armata/Moment/Getty Images; p. 5 Bettmann/Getty Images; pp. 7, 14, 22, 30, 41 cla78/Shutterstock.com; p. 8 Historical/Corbis Historical/Getty Images; p. 10 NurPhoto/Getty Images; p. 11 Samir Hussein/Redferns/Getty Images; p. 15 Stefano Blanchetti/Corbis Historical/Getty Images; p. 17 Fine Art/Corbis Historical/Getty Images; p. 20 ullstein bild/Getty Images; p. 23 Frederic J. Brown/AFP/Getty Images; p. 25 Jeff Greenberg/Universal Images Group/Getty Images; p. 27 Purestock/Getty Images; p. 31 De Agostini Picture Library/De Agostini/Getty Images; p. 35 Saul Loeb/AFP/Getty Images; p. 38 Pool/Getty Images; p. 40 Anadolu Agency/Getty Images; p. 42 FPG/Archive Photos/Getty Images; p. 44 Shepard Sherbell/Corbis Historical/Getty Images; p. 47 Randy Olson/NATIONAL GEOGRAPHIC IMAGE COLLECTION/Getty Images; p. 50 Yvonne Brandenberg/AFP/Getty Images.

Design: Michael Moy; Layout Design: Tahara Anderson; Editor: Bethany Bryan; Photo Research: Nicole Baker